AF506163

Adelaide
South Australia

Text by Cil Dobré

Photography by Pete Dobré

National Library of Australia Cataloguing-in-Publication Data:
Dobré, Cil.
Adelaide: South Australia
ISBN 0 9577063 9 1
1. Adelaide (S. Aust.) - Description and travel.
2. Adelaide (S. Aust.) - Pictorial works.
I. Dobré, Pete, 1958- . II. Title.
919.4231

Published and distributed by Pete Dobré's Oz Scapes
P.O. Box 305, Happy Valley, South Australia, 5159, Australia
Email: ozscapes@cobweb.com.au   Phone/Fax: +61 8 8381 5895
Website: www.petedobre.com

Special thanks to 'The Bear' and Ringa for their unconditional support and for the usage of their awesome dinghy.

Behind every act of creation lies the Creator.

Books Available in Panoramic Series

The Flinders Ranges,
South Australia

Arkaroola, Northern Flinders
Ranges, South Australia

The Cooper Creek in the
Australian Outback

Kangaroo Island, South Australia

The Strzelecki, Birdsville &
Oodnadatta Tracks in
Outback Australia

The Fleurieu Peninsula,
South Australia

The Simpson Desert
in Outback Australia

Adelaide

North
To the
Barossa Valley
Port Adelaide
To
Birdwood
Semaphore
North Adelaide
Morialta
Conservation
Park
Grange
Henley Beach
West Beach
Adelaide
GULF
ST VINCENT
Unley
The Summit
Cleland
Conservation
& Wildlife Park
Glenelg
RANGES
Brighton
LOFTY
To the
Monarto
Zoological Park
and Hahndorf
Hallett
Cove
MOUNT
To the
Fleurieu Peninsula
Port
Noarlunga

SOUTH AUSTRALIA
Adelaide

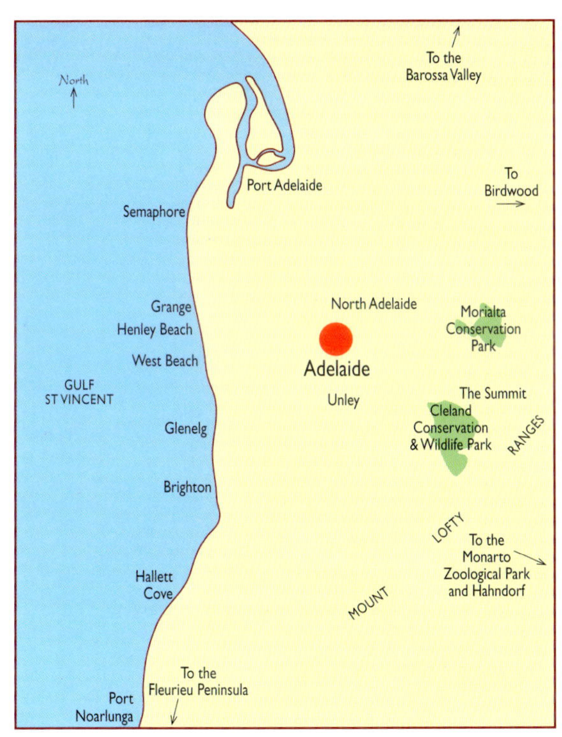

Adelaide

Adelaide, South Australia, is one of Australia's most pleasant cities.

This elegant city, cosmopolitan yet relaxed and comfortable is a political, judicial, cultural and commercial centre, providing convenient shopping in a compact area. Enjoy the space and fresh air and soak up the casual mood of this café society, as you stroll past grand buildings and through parklands, to appreciate the blend of old and new.

The Mt Lofty Ranges provide a picturesque backdrop to the city. A short drive from the city to Mt Lofty Summit offers panoramic views over Adelaide and the swimming beaches of Gulf St Vincent, stretching north and south.

Before Europeans settled in Adelaide, the Kaurna people lived here. This peaceful Aboriginal group worked skilfully with skins and fibres.

A scenic lookout on Montefiore Hill features a statue of Colonel Light, the first surveyor-general who planned Adelaide in 1836. Over a million Adelaidians can thank him for this well-planned city. The wide straight streets, with spacious squares, are surrounded by the space and beauty of open parklands, which separate the suburbs and industries. Wise planning makes the CBD accessible, with few traffic problems which ensures easy commuting.

Named after Queen Adelaide, this colony wasn't a penal dumping ground. Immigrants came with a different outlook. Copper was discovered, mines developed and Adelaide became a trans-shipment port for mining equipment and general supplies. Building and agriculture boomed. The River Murray opened to steam navigation. Paddle steamers and improved rail transportation allowed the eastern states' trades and riches to pour into South Australia. By the 1890's Adelaide blossomed into a gracious city. Her appearance changed little during the war years while post war years saw an era of industrial expansion.

Walk along North Terrace, with its major cultural institutions, to appreciate the attractive and varied Victorian architecture blending with contemporary style. Visit the Art Gallery of South Australia, the Museum, Adelaide University, Parliament House, the Adelaide Railway Station converted to a Casino, the Convention Centre and luxury hotels. See Adelaide's historic memorials, statues and plaques. Enjoy our heritage in stylish and ambient Adelaide Arcade, a 19th century shopping development. Appreciate the Town Hall, modelled on buildings in Genoa and Florence.

Adelaide Oval is known world-wide as the most picturesque Test Cricket ground. Also the parklands host many recreational pursuits, from rowing on the River Torrens, to tennis at Memorial Drive, golf courses, the Aquatic Centre at North Adelaide, and numerous sporting fields and courts. Football Park Stadium, Adelaide Super-Drome, ETSA Park and Hindmarsh Soccer Stadium provide world class sporting facilities in Adelaide.

Visit the National Wine Centre, to appreciate different Australian wines and wine regions. Experience an interactive journey through the past, present and future of the Australian wine industry. In the Tasting Gallery, you may taste an extensive selection of wines.

Enjoy walking through the Botanic Garden to visit the tropical rainforest in an interesting conservatory. Take a guided bird walk along the River Torrens. Ride Pop-Eye along the River Torrens, gliding under bridges, alongside parks, colourful gardens, boathouses and restaurants. Taste a 'pie floater' from a street cart in the evening. Wander around North Adelaide's historical buildings. Enjoy the Rose Gardens on South Terrace and the landscaped Adelaide Zoo, with many natural habitats. Walk Adelaide's streets with its multicultural nature as many migrants settle in Adelaide.

Known as the 'Festival City', Adelaide has world acclaim for its biennial Arts Festival. Arts flourish, history is appreciated with new ideas welcomed. Theatre, music, visual arts and drama are performed in theatres, on streets, in open-air locations, as well as unorthodox and unexpected venues.

Womadelaide attracts traditional, contemporary and indigenous musicians from around the world, to celebrate music in the green parklands.

View the Christmas Pageant, a colourful parade through Adelaide's streets, delighting tourists and locals.

A visit to the Adelaide Central Market is a gastronomical delight and a multicultural experience. Numerous traders sell the best range of fresh fruit, vegetables, seafood, meat and gourmet foods. Enjoy the sounds, vibrant colours and delicious aromas. The market is accessible to farmers and buyers.

Adelaide is famed as the city of restaurants. Whether it's the East End, Hutt, Gouger, O'Connell or Melbourne Street, you'll discover a dynamic café and dining culture. With a Mediterranean climate and warm dry summers and cool winters, it's perfect for alfresco dining for much of the year. Adelaide is known nationally and internationally for its culinary focus. Many tourists come for a food and wine experience.

Drive sixty minutes north of the city to Australia's famous wine producing area, the Barossa Valley, to enjoy fine wine, food and hospitality. Germanic influence in the Barossa is evident in the towns, shop names, buildings, high church steeples, menus in bakeries, restaurants and wineries, band music and festivals enjoyed in the valley.

Or head forty minutes south of Adelaide to the McLaren Vale Wine Region to taste rich, full flavoured, regional award winning wines.

Adelaide has wonderful suburbs nearby. Catch a tram to Glenelg, where the colony was proclaimed in 1836, to view the casual beach resort. In North Adelaide appreciate the blend of old and new. For upmarket shopping, sophistication and style, visit Norwood, Glenside, Unley and Hyde Park. Grange, Henley Beach and Semaphore offer seaside charm and come to Port Adelaide, a heritage area with its working fishing port.

Near Mt Lofty, twenty minutes from Adelaide, admire Australian wildlife in the natural bush setting at Cleland Wildlife Park. In the picturesque Adelaide Hills, discover market gardens, farmlets, orchards, vineyards, wineries and restaurants. See art and craft galleries scattered throughout the valleys, along with stately homes and cottages, surrounded by wonderful gum trees.

As a visitor or a resident, you will delight in this gracious well-planned city.

Skyline of Adelaide from the River Torrens

St Peter's Cathedral

Pop-Eye - River Torrens

Scenic Lookout at Montefiore Hill

Skyline of Adelaide featuring the Adelaide Convention Centre

Adelaide Skyline

Rundle Mall

Adelaide Oval

Adelaide Oval

Adelaide Central Market

Adelaide Central Market

Christmas Pageant

16

Christmas Pageant

Rundle Street Café Scene

Rundle Street Café Scene

Adelaide Railway Station

The Rotunda in Elder Park

Victoria Square

Adelaide University

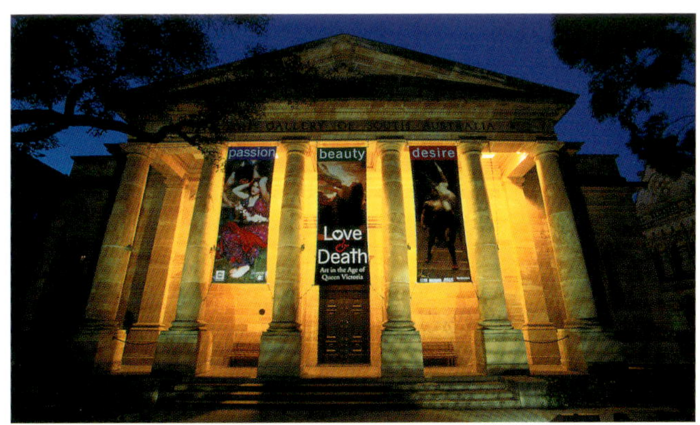

Art Gallery of South Australia

View over the National Wine Centre of Australia

The Interior of the National Wine Centre of Australia

National Wine Centre of Australia

National Wine Centre of Australia

The Bicentennial Conservatory and International Rose Garden in the Adelaide Botanic Garden

Adelaide Zoo

South Australian Museum

National Motor Museum – Birdwood

Glenelg

Glenelg

Carrick Hill

Carrick Hill

Port Adelaide

QE2 and the Aurora at Outer Harbor

Port Adelaide Lighthouse

Port Dock Station Railway Museum – Port Adelaide

South Australian Maritime Museum – Port Adelaide

Henley Jetty

Grange Jetty

Semaphore Jetty

Morialta Falls

Waterfall Gully

Winter

Piccadilly - Adelaide Hills

Kangaroos
Cleland Wildlife Park

42

Dingo

Tasmanian Devil

Koalas

Cleland Wildlife Park

Adelaide Hills

Hahndorf

Monarto Zoological Park

Monarto Zoological Park

Brighton Jetty

Port Noarlunga Jetty

Hallett Cove Conservation Park

The Sugarloaf - Hallett Cove Conservation Park

McLaren Vale - Fleurieu Peninsula

McLaren Vale Wine Region

Horse Tram travelling between Victor Harbor and Granite Island

Steam Ranger travelling along the Encounter Coast

Granite Island and Victor Harbor

The Bluff and Encounter Bay

The PS Oscar W - Goolwa

The Wooden Boat Festival - Goolwa - Fleurieu Peninsula

Murray Mouth – Fleurieu Peninsula

River Murray

River Murray

Remarkable Rocks - Kangaroo Island

Seal Bay – Kangaroo Island

Barossa Balloon Regatta

Chateau Yaldara – Barossa Valley

Barossa Valley

Aerial View of Adelaide